PEACHES!
PEACHES!
PEACHES!

by
Melissa Mosley

HEARTS 'N TUMMIES COOKBOOK COMPANY

a dinky division of Quixote Press

(800) 571 BOOK
(319) 372 7480

HEARTS 'N TUMMIES COOKBOOK COMPANY
1854 - 345th Ave.
Wever, IA 52658
800-571-2665

ISBN 1-57166-0887 $5.95

WHY COOKIN' WITH PEACHES!

This little cookbook includes a selection of recipes meant for enjoyment by all ages. There's nothing yummier than a fresh peach pie or cobbler. Try some of the sauces, jams and preserves. But, no matter how many recipes you try, peaches taste great.

Matthew, my second born, says they're great ripe off the peach tree. (He likes the juice to run down his chin, so Brutas our dog, can lick it off.)

TABLE OF CONTENTS

PEACH PIES AND CRUSTS

(more)

BEST EVER PIE CRUST

6 c. flour
1 T. salt
2 c. shortening or lard
1/2 c. margarine

2 T. vegetable oil
1 c. buttermilk
1 tsp. vanilla

Mix flour, salt, shortening, oil and margarine. Add buttermilk and vanilla. It rolls out very easy. Do not change ingredients; except vegetable shortening can be used instead of lard.

GRANDMA'S PIE CRUST

1 T. salt   1-1/2 c. flour
2/3 c. Crisco

Stir together and mix until flaky. Add 1/3 c. of cold water. Softly mix together. Makes top and bottom crust for a peach pie.

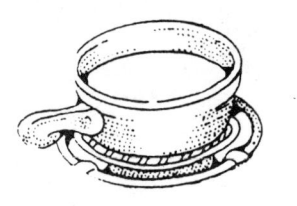

SIMPLY PIE CRUST

3 c. flour
1 tsp. salt
1 c. lard

1 egg (slightly beaten)
1/2 tsp. vinegar
5 T. ice water

Cut lard into flour and salt until particles are the size of peas. Mix in the egg, vinegar and ice water. Gather pastry into a bowl and roll out on floured pastry sheet. Makes 2 double crust pies.

BOATER'S PEACH PIE

(Preheat oven to 400°.)

3/4 c. sugar (can use 1/4 c. brown
  sugar for part of the 3/4 c.)
2 to 3 T. flour
1/4 tsp. cinnamon

5 c. peeled, sliced fresh peaches
2 T. butter or margarine
1 pastry shell
Pastry for lattice top

Combine sugar, flour and cinnamon; add to peaches and mix lightly.
Spread into a 9-inch pastry shell. Dot with butter before or after adjusting lattice top. Flute the edges. If you prefer a full top crust, you can
sprinkle top with sugar. Bake in hot oven for 45 to 50 minutes. Cool
before cutting.

CREAMY PEACH PIE

(Preheat oven to 400°.)

3 c. peeled and sliced peaches
3/4 c. white sugar
1/4 c. flour

1/4 tsp. salt
1/4 tsp. nutmeg
1 c. whipping cream

Prepare 9-inch unbaked pastry shell. Add above mixture to peaches. Toss lightly. Turn into pastry shell. Pour 1 c. whipping cream over top of peaches. Bake for 35 to 45 minutes.

CRUMBLY PEACH PIE

(Preheat oven to 350°.)

1 c. sugar
1/2 c. flour
1/4 tsp. nutmeg
1/4 c. water

1/4 c. butter
6-8 large fresh peaches
1/2 recipe plain pastry

Mix sugar, flour and nutmeg. Cut in butter until crumbly. Sprinkle half the crumb mixture in a 9-inch pastry lined pie pan. Slice peaches over mixture, then add remaining crumb mixture. Pour water over pie. Bake until done.

FRESH JUICY PEACH PIE

5 T. peach Jello
3 T. cornstarch
1 c. sugar

3/4 c. water
3 fresh peaches
1 baked 9-inch pie shell

Boil Jello, cornstarch, sugar and water until thick and clear. Cool. Line pie shell with a little of the pudding. Slice fresh peaches into pie shell. Cover with pudding. Refrigerate.

FRESH PEACH PIE

| 1 c. sugar | 2 T. cornstarch |
| 1 c. water | 3 peaches |

Boil above, stirring constantly until thick and clear. Then dissolve 1/2 pkg. (3 T.) peach Jello in above mixture. Let this cool, but not set. Put a coat of this mixture in baked pie shell, slice peaches in a layer, add more Jello mixture, then layer of peaches and end with Jello mixture. Be sure peaches are covered. Set in refrigerator. Put whipped cream on top. Use Fruit Fresh in peaches to keep color if desired.

FRESH PEACH NUT PIE

1 (3 oz.) pkg. peach Jello
2 T. (rounded) cornstarch
1/3 c. sugar
1 c. water

3 c. diced peaches
1 c. flour
1 stick margarine
1/2 c. chopped nuts

Heat first 4 ingredients until thick or clear. Cool. Add 3 c. diced peaches. For the crust, mix flour, margarine and nuts and press in a 9-inch pie pan. Bake crust for 20 minutes at 350°. Cool crust and pour Jello mixture in it. Top with Cool Whip and refrigerate.

GLAZED PEACH PIE

3 T. cornstarch
1 c. sugar
1/2 c. water
1 c. mashed fresh peaches

1 T. butter or margarine
1 9-inch baked pie shell
3 c. sliced fresh peaches
Sweetened whipped cream

Combine cornstarch and sugar, then add water and mix well. Add the 1 c. crushed peaches. Bring to a boil and cook over low heat until clear. Add butter or margarine and cool slightly. Line baked pie shell with fresh sliced peaches. Spread on filling. Chill for 2 hours. Serve with a dip of ice cream or whipped cream is good also.

GOLDEN PEACH PIE

(Preheat oven to 375°.)

1 lb. peaches	2 T. flour
1/3 c. peach juice	2 T. lemon juice
1/2 c. sugar	1/8 tsp. almond extract
1/4 tsp. nutmeg	2 T. butter

Cook and stir until mixture thickens. Pour into 9-inch pie crust. Add top crust. Bake for 40 to 45 minutes.

GRANDMA'S CREAM PEACH PIE

(Preheat oven to 350°.)

1 unbaked pie shell	2 skimpy layers sliced peaches
3/4 c. sugar	3 T. flour
3/4 c. Half and Half	

Mix 3/4 c. sugar and 3 T. flour. Sprinkle this mixture over peaches. Pour 3/4 c. Half and Half over all. Sprinkle nutmeg on top. Bake for 45 minutes.

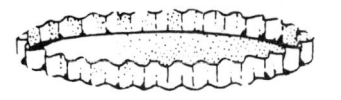

GRANDMA'S PEACH PIE

(Preheat oven to 350°.)

1 pie shell (9 or 10-inch)   5 or 6 peeled peaches
2 T. flour (sprinkled on bottom of crust)

SAUCE:
3/4 c. sugar   1 egg
1 tsp. vanilla   2 T. flour
3/4 stick butter

Start with pie shell, put 2 T. flour in the bottom of pie shell, then cover shell with peaches. To make sauce combine all other ingredients in pan until it becomes creamy; pour over peaches. Bake for 1 hour.

LAZY PEACH PIE

(Preheat oven to 350°.)

1/2 c. butter or margarine	1/2 tsp. salt
1 c. flour	3/4 c. milk
1 c. sugar	1 tsp. vanilla
1 tsp. baking powder	1 can peaches

Melt butter or margarine in oblong cake pan. Mix together flour, sugar, baking powder, salt, milk and vanilla. Pour into buttered pan. Pour peaches and juice over batter, arranging peaches neatly. Bake for 1 hour.

OPEN FACE PEACH PIE

(Preheat oven to 400°.)

1 c. sugar
1/3 c. flour

1/4 c. butter
Peach halves

Crumb together the sugar, flour and butter. Put 1/2 of the crumbs in the bottom of pie plate. Place peach halves (rounded side up) over crumbs, using 1 layer of peaches. Put remaining crumbs on top. Bake at 400° for 35 minutes.

22

PEACH CHOCOLATE CRUST PIE

1-1/3 c. condensed milk - sweet
1/4 c. lemon juice
Chocolate wafers

1 c. peaches - large
Whipped cream

Blend lemon juice with condensed milk. Add fresh sliced peaches. Pour into pie plate which has been lined with ground chocolate wafers (about 3/4 c. for average pie pan). Cut enough wafers into halves to stand around the edge of the pie. Put whipped cream on top and chill in refrigerator.

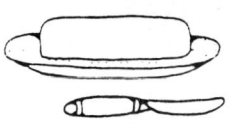

PEACH CREAM PIE

(Preheat oven to 350°.)

3 peaches (sliced thin)
1 c. sugar
4 T. flour
1/2 tsp. vanilla

Dash of salt
1/2 c. whipping cream
1/2 c. Half and Half

Mix dry ingredients together first. Add rest of ingredients. Lay peaches on bottom of crust. Pour cream mixture over peaches. Bake for approximately 45 minutes or until firm.

PEACH CUSTARD PIE

(Preheat oven to 400°.)

1 c. sugar
2 T. flour
2 T. butter

2 eggs (well beaten)
1 c. sliced peaches

Line unbaked crust with peach slices. Cream sugar, flour and butter together. Add eggs and pour over peaches. Bake for 15 minutes; reduce heat to 325° and bake another 45 minutes.

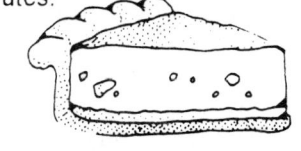

PEACH ICE CREAM PIE

1/2 c. butter or margarine
1/2 c. brown sugar
1-1/2 c. oatmeal
2/3 c. almonds

1 (3 oz.) pkg. orange gelatin
1 c. boiling water
2 c. vanilla ice cream
2 c. diced peaches

Toast oatmeal in 350° oven for 5 minutes: add almonds and toast for 5 minutes more. Remove from oven and add melted butter or margarine and brown sugar. Line a pie tin and chill. Reserve 1/2 c. of mixture for top. Mix orange gelatin and the 1 c. boiling water; add the 2 c. vanilla ice cream and 2 c. diced peaches. Refrigerate until slightly thickened and fill oatmeal crust. Sprinkle remaining crumbs on top and refrigerate.

PEACH PIE

1 baked pie shell
1 c. sugar
2 T. cornstarch
1 c. water

Yellow food coloring
3 T. peach Jello
Peaches
Cool Whip

For the filling, mix sugar, cornstarch and water. Cook until clear, then add 5 to 6 drops yellow food coloring. Add 3 T. peach Jello. Slice fresh peaches and put in crust. Pour cooled glaze over top and refrigerate. Serve with Cool Whip if desired.

PEACH PIE ALASKA

1 (3 oz.) pkg. Jello
  (lemon, orange or peach)
1 baked 9-inch pie crust
2/3 c. boiling water

1 c. vanilla ice cream
1 c. diced fresh peaches
3-1/2 c. Cool Whip (thawed)

Dissolve Jello in boiling water. Add ice cream by the spoonfuls. Stir until melted and smooth. Blend in Cool Whip and fruit. Chill, if necessary, until mixture will mound. Spoon into crust. Chill about 3 hours or freeze until firm. Serves 8.

PEACH TAPIOCA PIE

(Preheat oven to 450°.)

6 c. sliced peaches
3 T. minute tapioca

3/4 c. sugar or more
3/4 tsp. lemon juice

Mix and set aside for 15 minutes.

3/4 c. flour

1/2 c. brown sugar

Crumble together and add 3/4 c. chopped pecans and 6 T. butter or margarine; mix. Put 1/3 of the crumbs in unbaked pie shell. Pour in fruit mixture and top with rest of crumbs. Bake for 10 minutes. Then turn oven down to 350° until done, about 45 minutes. This recipe is for a large Corning Ware pie plate or a ready-made frozen deep dish pie crust.

PEACHY CREAM PIE

6 peaches	1/3 c. flour
2 eggs	1/4 tsp. salt
1/2 c. sugar	2 c. milk, scalded
Cream	Lemon extract

Mix the sugar, sifted flour and salt together; add to the beaten eggs. Blend with the scalded milk and cook for fifteen minutes, stirring constantly; add flavoring. When cool pour over sliced peaches which have been put in a baked pastry shell and top all with whipped cream.

NO BAKE PEACH PIE

CRUST:
1-1/2 c. almonds

1-1/4 c. dates, pitted

FILLING:
6 c. peaches, sliced
1/4 tsp. almond extract

1 T. maple syrup
2 T. shredded coconut

CRUST: Grind the almonds and set aside. Grind the dates to form a paste. Add the ground almonds and form a ball. Press into an 8-inch pie plate. Refrigerate until ready to fill.

FILLING: Toss the peaches with the maple syrup and almond extract. Spoon into the pie crust and sprinkle with the shredded coconut. Serve.

PEACH COBBLERS

EASY PEACH COBBLER

(Preheat oven to 350°.)

1 c. flour
1 c. sugar
Pinch of salt
2 T. baking powder

1 stick of butter
1 quart peaches
Scant cup of milk

Melt butter in a 9x13-inch baking pan. Mix up a batter of flour, sugar, baking powder and enough milk to make a thin batter and pour over melted butter in pan. Carefully place peaches over the batter. Bake until done. Serves 6 to 8.

EASIER PEACH COBBLER

(Preheat oven to 325°.)

1/2 c. butter or margarine
1 c. sugar
1 c. flour

2/3 c. milk
1 qt. fresh peaches
1 tsp. baking powder

Melt butter. Combine sugar, flour, baking powder and milk in mixing bowl; mix well. Pour melted butter over sugar mixture. Do not stir. Arrange peaches in 9x13-inch baking pan. Pour sugar mixture over top. Bake for 30 minutes or until done.

EASIEST PEACH COBBLER

(Preheat oven to 350°.)

8 oz. sliced peaches
   (juice and all)
1 T. chopped pecans

Butter brickle cake mix
1 stick of butter

Put in a 9x13-inch pan. Sprinkle a butter brickle (dry) cake mix over the peaches. Dot with 1 stick of butter over the top. Sprinkle pecans on top. Bake for 50 minutes.

FRESH PEACH COBBLER

(Preheat oven to 325°.)

1 c. sugar	1/2 c. sifted cake flour
1/4 tsp. salt	2 eggs
2 T. quick cooking tapioca	1/4 tsp. cream of tartar
4 c. fresh peaches	1/8 tsp. salt & dash cinnamon
1 c. water	1/2 c. sugar

Combine 1 cup of sugar, salt, cinnamon, tapioca, peaches and water in a saucepan. Cook and stir until it comes to a boil. Pour into a 2-quart baking dish. Sift flour once, measure: combine eggs, cream of tartar and salt and beat until foamy, then gradually add sugar and beat until thick and lemon colored. Gradually fold in flour. Pour over hot fruit mixture. Bake for 1 hour or until done. Serves 6-8.

GRANDMA'S PEACH COBBLER

(Preheat oven to 450°.)

Have an 8 or 9-inch square pan ready. Combine in a mixing bowl:

1 c. flour	1 c. sugar
1 tsp. baking powder	1/2 tsp. salt

Cut in 2 T. shortening. Set aside. In a non-corrosive saucepan, combine:

2 to 3 c. sliced peaches	1/2 c. water
3/4 c. sugar	

Bring to a boil. While the fruit heats up, stir into the dry ingredients 1/2 c. milk. Pour the batter into the pan and put the boiling fruit over it. Bake 10 minutes, then decrease heat to 350° and cook about another 15 minutes. Serve warm (or eat cold for breakfast).

MAGIC PEACH COBBLER

(Preheat oven to 350°.)

1 stick oleo or butter
1 c. flour
1 c. sugar
1-1/2 tsp. baking powder

3/4 c. milk
1/2 c. sugar
2 c. peaches

Melt butter in 9x13-inch pan or dish. Mix first four ingredients and pour over butter. No not stir. Add 2 c. peaches with juice. Sprinkle remaining 1/2 c. sugar over peaches. Bake for 30 minutes.

MOM'S PEACH COBBLER

(Preheat oven to 400°.)

1/4 c. butter
4 c. peaches (peeled & sliced)
1/2 c. sugar
1 T. + 2/3 c. variety baking mix

1/2 tsp. ground cinnamon
2 T. brown sugar
2 T. milk

In 1-quart casserole, combine peaches, sugar, 1 T. baking mix and cinnamon. In medium bowl, mix remaining 2/3 c. baking mix with brown sugar. Cut in butter until mixture is size of small peas. Stir in milk until moistened; drop by spoonfuls onto peaches. Bake for 30 minutes or until toothpick comes clean. Let stand 5 minutes. Serves 6.

MORE PEACH COBBLER

(Preheat oven to 350°.)

Butter a shallow ceramic baking dish or a 9-inch tart pan.

Combine in a mixing bowl:

1 c. milk	1/4 c. heavy cream
1/4 c. sugar	3 eggs
1 T. vanilla	1/8 tsp. salt
2/3 c. flour	

Beat until foamy. Pour 1/4 batter into the buttered dish. Bake 2 minutes until just barely set. Arrange 10 medium peaches, skinned, pitted, halves, cut side down in the dish and pour the remaining batter over them. Bake 30 to 35 minutes until custard is puffed and brown. Dust with powdered sugar. Serve warm.

PEACH COBBLER

(Preheat oven to 350°.)

4 c. sliced peaches
2 T. oleo or butter
1/2 c. sugar
1/2 c. water
2 T. flour
1 tsp. cinnamon

(more)

2 c. flour
3 tsp. baking powder
1/4 tsp. salt
4 T. shortening
3/4 c. milk
1 egg

Blend peaches, oleo, sugar, water, flour and cinnamon. Pour into shallow greased pan. To make crust: Mix flour, baking powder, salt. Work in shortening. Add milk and egg. Spread soft mixture over peaches. Leave holes in top. Bake 1/2 hour or more in moderate oven. Pour over this syrup when taken from oven: 1/2 c. sugar and 1/2 c. water. Bring to boil 2 minutes. Pour over cobbler and bake 5 minutes more. Serve warm. Good with milk or scoop ice cream on top.

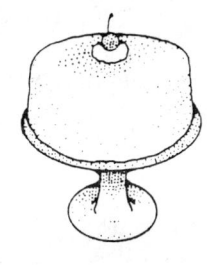

PEACHY COBBLER

(Preheat oven to 375°.)

1/3 c. oleo/butter flavor Crisco
1 c. flour
Pinch salt
5 c. peaches

1/2 c. sugar
1 tsp. baking powder
1/2 c. milk
Sugar

Cream oleo and sugar. Mix flour, baking powder and salt. Cut into oleo/sugar mixture using fork or pastry cutter. Stir in milk. Mix and put in bottom of greased small brownie pan. Peel peaches, slice them into thin 1-inch slices. Add enough sugar to make them sweet, mash slightly. Pour on top of cobbler crust. Bake until slightly brown.

QUICK EASY PEACH COBBLER

5 to 8 fresh peaches
2 c. sugar

2 sticks butter (melted)
10 slices white bread
(edges off)

Peel peaches, cover bottom of pan with peaches, put bread over peaches. Mix together sugar, flour and melted butter. Pour over bread and peaches. Bake at 350° until bread is brown.

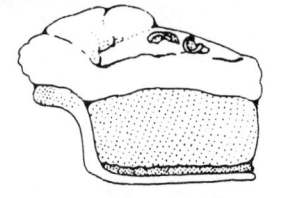

QUICK PEACH COBBLER

4 c. sliced fresh peaches
1-1/2 c. sugar
3/4 c. flour

2 tsp. baking powder
3/4 c. milk
1/4 c. butter or oleo

Mix peaches with 1 c. sugar. Set oven to 350°. Put butter in 8x8-inch baking dish (or 8x12-inch dish). Set dish in oven to melt butter. Make batter of sugar, flour, baking powder and milk. Pour over melted butter. Do not stir. Pour peaches over batter. Do not stir. Bake for 45 minutes.

PEACH CAKES

CAKE WITH PEACHES

1 white cake mix, prepared
   as directed
1 large box cherry or
   strawberry Jello

2 c. boiling water
1 pkg. Dream Whip
Sliced peaches

Dissolve Jello in boiling water and pour over perforated cake when done. (Punch holes in cake to perforate and pour Jello over while cake is still warm.) Chill in refrigerator.

Mix peaches into whipped cream and serve as topping or mix 1 box pudding already prepared with whipped cream and decorate with sliced peaches.

CURRIED FRUIT CAKE

(Preheat oven to 325°.)

8 oz. pear halves
8 oz. peach halves
8 oz. apricot halves
8 oz. pineapple spears
  (cut up)

1 small jar maraschino cherries
3/4 c. brown sugar
1/2 c. melted butter
Dash of curry powder
1/4 c. apricot brandy

Drain all fruits and arrange in casserole or flat baking dish. Mix together curry powder, brown sugar and butter. Pour over fruit and bake 1 hour in 325° oven. Dish can be left in oven (turned off) for 2 to 3 hours. Good served with ham or chicken.

FRUIT COFFEE CAKE

(Preheat oven to 375°.)

2 T. vegetable shortening
4 T. sugar
1 egg
1-2/3 c. flour (sifted)
1/2 c. milk

1/4 tsp. salt
1 tsp. vanilla
1 c. sweetened cooked peaches
3 T. baking powder

Topping:
1 T. butter (melt over hot water)
1/4 c. flour (sifted)
1/2 tsp. vanilla

1/2 c. sugar
2 T. cinnamon

Cream together the shortening, sugar; add the egg and beat. Sift together the dry ingredients. Add vanilla. Place in oiled pan and cover the dough. Add the fruit, adding a few drops of lemon extract to bring out the flavor. Blend all the topping ingredients thoroughly and spread over the dough. Bake 30 minutes at 375°.

OLD FASHIONED PEACH CAKE

(Preheat oven to 350°.)

1 box yellow cake mix
3 eggs
8 oz. peach pie filling
1/2 c. nuts

1 stick butter
1 c. sugar
1 c. flour

Mix together cake mix, eggs, pie filling and nuts. Pour into greased and floured 9x13-inch pan. Mix together butter, sugar and flour with a fork until blended. Sprinkle over cake and bake at 350° for 40 to 45 minutes.

PEACH ANGEL CAKE

2 T. (2 env.) plain gelatin
1/2 c. cold water
6 beaten egg whites
3/4 c. sugar
1/4 tsp. salt
6 beaten egg whites

(more)

1/2 c. lemon juice
1-1/2 T. grated lemon rind
3/4 c. sugar
2 c. crushed peaches
1 angel food cake

(continued)

Soften gelatin in cup of water. Combine egg yolks with 3/4 c. sugar and salt. Stir in lemon juice. Cook over hot water until coats a spoon, stirring constantly to prevent curdling. Remove from heat. Add lemon rind and softened gelatin. Stir until gelatin is melted and dissolved. Gradually beat 3/4 c. sugar into beaten egg whites. Fold egg whites and crushed peaches into custard. Break angel food cake into bite size pieces. In greased angel food pan alternate layers of cake and peaches mixture. Chill until firm. Serve with whipped cream and garnish with peach slices.

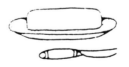

PEACH CAKE

(Preheat oven to 350°.)

8 oz. peach slices   1-1/2 sticks margarine
1 pkg. yellow or white cake mix

Put peaches with juice in greased cake pan. Sprinkle dry cake mix over top. Drizzle melted margarine over top. Bake for 40 to 45 minutes in a 9x13-inch pan.

55

PEACH CAKE WITH FROSTING

(Preheat oven to 350°)

1 c. shortening or oil
2 c. sugar
2 eggs
2 c. chopped or mashed
   fresh peaches (heated)
2 tsp. soda

2 c. flour
1 tsp. salt
1 tsp. allspice
1 tsp. cinnamon
1 tsp. cloves
2 tsp. cocoa

Beat together oil, sugar and eggs. Then add peaches. Sift together flour,
salt, allspice, cinnamon. cloves, soda and cocoa. Add to other mixture
and mix well. Bake in a sheet cake for 30 minutes.

(more)

(continued)

FROSTING:

1 stick butter or margarine	1/4 c. milk
1 c. brown sugar	1-3/4 c. sifted powdered sugar

Boil in saucepan butter and brown sugar. Then add milk and bring to a boil. Remove from heat and cool to lukewarm. Add the powdered sugar. Beat until smooth. Spread over cake. Delicious!

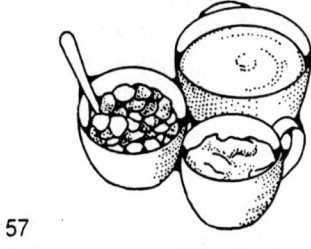

PEACH CARAMEL CAKE

(Preheat oven to 350°.)

1/3 c. brown sugar
2 T. water
1 T. butter or oleo

3 big ripe peaches or 6 canned halves (sliced)

Cake Batter

1/2 c. milk
1 T. butter
2 eggs
1/2 c. granulated sugar
1/2 c. brown sugar

1 tsp. baking powder
1 c. sifted flour
1/4 tsp. salt
1 tsp. vanilla

(more)

58

(continued)

In baking pan, 8x8x2-inches, stir together the 1/3 c. sugar, water and butter. Heat this mixture until smooth. Arrange the peach slices evenly in this mixture. Set aside while preparing cake batter. Measure into sifter the flour, baking powder and salt. In small saucepan heat to boiling the 1/2 c. milk, 1 T. butter. Beat the eggs and gradually add the granulated sugar and brown sugar. Continue beating until thick and well mixed. Add sifted dry ingredients alternately with hot milk mixture. Add vanilla. Stir until batter is smooth: pour over peaches in pan. Bake for 45 minutes or until toothpick comes clean when tested. Serves 6-8.

PEACHY CINNAMON COFFEE CAKE

(Preheat oven to 400°.)

1 pkg. bakery style cinnamon
  swirl with crumb
  topping muffin mix

8-1/4 oz. juice packed
  peaches
1 egg

Grease 8 or 9-inch round pan. Drain peaches reserving juice. Add enough water to juice to make 3/4 c. Combine muffin mix, egg and juice mixture in medium bowl. Pour into pan. Knead swirl packet 10 seconds before opening. Squeeze contents on top of batter and swirl with knife. Sprinkle topping over batter. Bake for 20 to 25 minutes or until golden. Serve warm - very good!

PEACH COFFEE CAKE

(Preheat oven to 350°.)

8 oz. peach pie filling
  (see pgs. 15 & 27)
2 tsp. ground cinnamon
3 c. flour
1 c. sugar
1-1/2 c. milk
1/2 c. softened butter

3 tsp. baking powder
1 tsp. salt
3 eggs
1/4 c. packed brown sugar
1/4 c. chopped nuts
2 T. butter, melted

(more)

61

(continued)

Spray 13x9x2-inch pan with no-stick coating. Mix pie filling and cinnamon; reserve. Beat flour, sugar, milk, butter, baking powder, salt and eggs in large bowl on low speed, scraping bowl constantly for 30 seconds. Beat on medium speed, scraping bowl frequently for 2 minutes. Pour half of batter into pan. Spoon half of pie filling mixture (1 cup) over batter in pan; repeat with remaining batter and pie filling mixture. Sprinkle brown sugar and nuts over pie filling mixture. Drizzle with melted butter. Bake until wooden pick inserted in center comes out clean for 40 to 50 minutes. Makes 12 to 16 servings. Serve warm, if possible.

PEACH CUSTARD CAKE

(Preheat oven to 375°.)

1-1/2 c. flour
1/2 tsp. salt
1/2 c. soft margarine
1 can sliced peaches
1 c. evaporated milk

1/2 c. sugar
1/2 tsp. cinnamon
1/2 c. peach syrup
1 egg

(more)

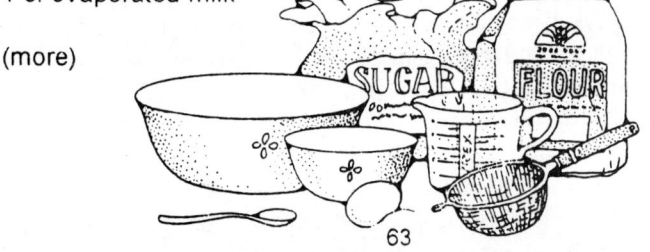

63

(continued)

Mix the flour, salt and oleo with pastry blender or two knives, until mixture looks like coarse meal. Press firmly on bottom and halfway up sides of buttered 8-inch baking dish. Drain peaches well, reserving 1/2 c. syrup. Arrange well-drained peach slices on crust in pan. Sprinkle over the peaches the sugar and cinnamon mixture. Bake in 375° oven for 20 minutes, then add custard, made as follows. Mix the peach syrup, 1 beaten egg and evaporated milk. Pour over peach and crust mixture, return to oven and bake 30 minutes more or until custard is firm except in center. Center becomes firm on standing. Serve warm or cold. Serves 9.

PEACH SOUR CREAM UPSIDE-DOWN CAKE

(Preheat oven to 375°.)

For topping:
1-1/2 lbs. firm just ripe yellow
  peaches (about 3-4)

1 stick unsalted butter
1/2 c. sugar

For cake batter:
Stir together and set aside:
1-1/2 c. all purpose flour
3/4 tsp. salt

1-1/2 tsp. baking powder

(more)

(continued)

Beat together:
1 stick unsalted butter, softened
2 tsp. fresh ginger, grated
(on a ginger grater)

1/2 c. sugar
1 tsp. vanilla

Add one at a time:
2 large eggs

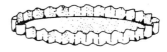

Stir in:
1/2 c. sour cream (or plain yogurt)
Gradually add flour mixture until
just combined.

(more)

Stir in: 1/2 a peach, peeled and chopped fine (try to include the juice). To prepare the topping, peel and quarter the peaches. In an ovenproof 10" skillet, melt the butter over low heat and stir in the sugar until dissolved. Place the peach quarters on their tummies in the butter and sugar, and let the mixture cook over very low heat until the sugar darkens and the peaches are soft, about 30 minutes.

While the topping cooks, prepare the cake.

When the peaches are ready and the cake batter is mixed, take the skillet off the heat and spoon the batter over the peaches, leaving a 1/2'" border uncovered around the edges (the cake will expand to cover the whole top). Bake at 375° for about 30 minutes or until the cake tests done. Cool 10 minutes, run a knife around the rim to loosen, then carefully invert onto a plate. Serve warm with vanilla ice cream.

PEACH UPSIDE DOWN CAKE

(Preheat oven to 350°.)

1 c. brown sugar
1/2 c. milk
1 c. white sugar
1/2 c. Crisco
1 egg

1-1/2 c. flour
2 tsp. baking powder
1/4 tsp. salt
1 tsp. vanilla
Peaches (5 cups or more)

Place brown sugar and Crisco in large iron skillet. When melted, place in pan as many sliced or halved peaches as possible. Pour the cake mixture over peaches. Bake for 40 minutes. Turn out on cake plate, peach side up. May be served with whipped cream.

PEACH UPSIDE-DOWN PUDDING CAKE

(Preheat oven to 350°.)

1/4 c. melted oleo
1/3 c. firmly packed brown sugar
29 oz. drained sliced peaches
1 pkg. yellow cake mix
4 eggs

1 c. sour cream
1/4 c. oil
1/2 tsp. almond extract
1 (3 oz.) pkg. vanilla
    flavor instant pudding mix

Combine butter and sugar; pour into a 9x13-inch pan. Arrange peaches on sugar mix. Combine remaining ingredients in large mixer bowl. Blend, then beat at medium speed 4 minutes. Spoon carefully into pan over peaches. Bake for 50 to 55 minutes or until cake springs back when lightly touched. Cool in pan 5 minutes. Invert onto platter; remove pan. May add whipped cream or ice cream over top.

PEACH PRESERVES, CONSERVES & JAMS

71

EASY PEACH PRESERVES

3/4 lb. sugar   1 lb. ripe peaches
3/4 c. water

Wash, peel, remove stones and cut peaches into quarters. Boil sugar and water 10 minutes. Skim. Add fruit and cook quickly until transparent. Seal in hot sterilized jars.

PEACH PRESERVES

Low Calorie

2-1/2 to 3 lbs. ripe peaches
(10 to 12)
24 packets non-sugar sweetener
or 7-1/4 tsp. non-sugar
sweetener

2 T. lemon juice
1 3/4 oz. pkg. pectin for
low-sugar preserves (low-
methoxyl pectin)

(more)

(continued)

Peel, pit and finely chop peaches; measure 4 cups into a large bowl. Stir in lemon juice and pectin. Let mixture stand 10 minutes, stirring frequently. Transfer to a large saucepan. Cook and stir over medium heat until mixture comes to a boil. Cook and stir 1 minute more. Remove from heat. Stir in non-sugar sweetener. Skim off foam, if necessary.

Ladle at once into freezer containers or jars, leaving 1/2-inch head space. Seal, label. Let stand at room temperature 4 to 6 hours or until set. Store up to 3 weeks in the refrigerator or 6 months in the freezer. Makes 4 cups (64 1-tablespoon servings).

PEACH & APRICOT PRESERVE

3 c. peaches, peeled & chopped
3 c. apricots, chopped
2 c. Shiro plums, sliced

2 T. lemon juice
6 c. sugar
1 T. margarine

In a dutch oven, combine 2 c. each of the peaches and apricots with the remaining ingredients excepting the margarine. Mash enough to break the fruit. Stir in the remaining peaches & apricots. Add margarine. Bring to a slow boil, stirring. Boil, continuing to stir frequently, for 20 minutes or until setting point is reached. Ladle into sterile 250ml canning jars leaving 1/2" head space. Wipe rim and seal. Process for 5 minutes in a boiling water bath. Remove, cool, label and store.

PEACH PRESERVES, MATTHEW'S FAVORITE

1 large peach orchard
2 small dogs
1 new kitten

1/2 dozen children
A pinch of brook
Some pebbles

Mix the children, the dogs and kitten together and put them in the peach orchard, stirring constantly. Pour the brook over the pebbles. Sprinkle the peach orchard with flowers. Spread over all a deep blue sky. Bake in a hot sun. When brown remove and set away to cool in a bathtub.

PEACH APPLE CONSERVE

2 c. peeled & chopped peaches
2 c. unpeeled & chopped
  red apple
3 c. sugar

2 T. maraschino cherries,
  minced
1/2 c. fresh lemon juice

Combine all ingredients in heavy saucepan. Cook over low heat 20 to 30 minutes until apples are transparent. Pour into hot sterilized jars and seal at once.

PEACH ORANGE CONSERVE

3 cut oranges
Grated rind of 1/2 orange
    and 1/2 lemon

12 peaches
Little lemon juice
3-1/2 lbs. sugar

Skin and slice peaches. Slice lemon and orange thin and lengthwise.
Boil lemon and orange with a little peach juice, about 30 minutes. Add
peaches taking one part fruit to one sugar. Cook about 30 minutes.
Drain through colander and cook juice to desired thickness. Add peaches
last 5 minutes; in a way fruit is not overcooked.

PEACH CHERRY NUT CONSERVE

3 lbs. sugar
25 peaches
1 c. walnuts

3 large oranges,
juice and rind
1/2 pint bottle maraschino cherries

Peel the peaches and remove the pits; cut into small pieces. Add sugar, oranges, grated rind and juice. Then heat slowly and boil gently for about an hour. Add nuts and cherries just before removing from the fire.

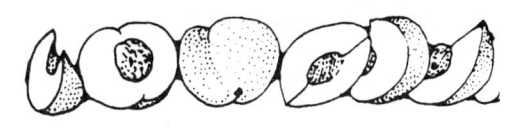

PEACH VINEGAR CONSERVE

8 lbs. peaches
6 lbs. sugar

1 pint vinegar

Put 2 to 3 cloves into each peach and add a few sticks of cinnamon to the water in which the peaches are cooked. Remove peaches to a platter to cool. Add the vinegar and sugar to the liquid left in the kettle. Cook until the syrup is heavy; then allow it to cool. When cold, pour the syrup over the peaches and let it stand for 24 hours before sealing.

PEACH SOUTHERN CONSERVE

5 c. ripe peaches, coarsely chopped
2 c. sugar
1 med. orange, seeded & chopped

1/4 lemon, seeded & chopped
1/2 c. seedless raisins
1/2 c. pecans, chopped

Place peaches in a heavy enamelized saucepan. Add sugar, chopped orange and juice, and chopped lemon and juice; mix to blend and let stand 1-2 hours. Place over low heat and cook until fruit gives off quite a bit of juice. Bring to a boil, reduce heat and let simmer, stirring often, until very thick. Stir in pecans and cook 5 minutes longer. Seal in hot sterilized jars.

FROZEN PEACH JAM

3 c. ground peaches   5-1/2 c. sugar

Combine and let stand 20 minutes. Mix 1 box Sure-Jell in 1 c. water. Bring to a boil and boil for 1 minute. Add the peaches and stir. Let stand 24 hours, then freeze.

PEACH JAM

5 c. crushed peaches   1 (No. 2-1/2) can crushed pineapple
7 c. sugar   2 (3 oz.) boxes strawberry gelatin

Combine peaches, sugar and pineapple. Boil for 15 minutes, then add gelatin, stirring until dissolved. Pour into jars and seal.

PEACH MARMALADE

6 pints peaches
1 pint water

3 pints granulated sugar

Pare peaches, cut in halves, remove pits. Measure fruit, place in kettle and add water. Cook nearly 1 hour. Add sugar and cook until thick and smooth.

PEACH BUTTERSCOTCH JAM

1-1/4 lbs. fully ripe peaches
  or 4 peaches
2 T. lemon juice (1 lemon)
1 tsp. ascorbic acid crystals
  (optional)

1/4 c. firmly packed brown sugar
3/4 c. water
1 (1-3/4 oz.) box powdered fruit
  pectin
4 c. sugar

Wash, scald and drain containers (5 to 6 jelly jars) and lids. Chop peaches. Measure 1-3/4 c. into large bowl or pan. Squeeze juice from 1 lemon. Measure 2 T. and add to fruit with ascorbic acid. Thoroughly mix sugars into fruit; set aside. Mix water and fruit pectin in small saucepan. Bring to boil and boil 1 minute, stirring constantly. Stir into fruit. Continue stirring about 3 minutes (a few sugar crystals will remain). Ladle quickly into jars. Cover at once with tight lids. Let stand at room temperature until set (may take up to 24 hours). Then store in freezer.

PEACH-PLUM JAM

Wash, peel and pit 4 cups peaches and 5 cups red plums. Cut fruit into small pieces and place in a large kettle. Add 8 cups sugar and one thinly sliced lemon, stirring well into mix. Boil rapidly, stirring constantly until jellying point is reached, or until thick. Remove from heat; skim and stir alternately for 5 minutes. Ladle into hot jars; seal. Yield: 12 half pints. The blending of the two fruit flavors and lemon is the secret of the wonderful flavor.

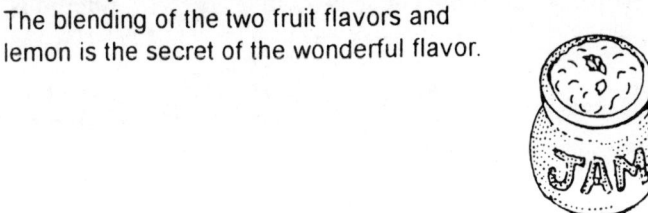

PEACH SAUCES, RELISH, PICKLES, BUTTER

GINGER PEACH CHUTNEY

Makes 6 to 8 cups. Serves 12.

7 c. peaches, peeled & sliced
2 T. coarse pickling salt
3 c. granulated sugar
1-1/2 c. cider vinegar
3 garlic cloves, minced
1/2 c. candied ginger, chopped

1 c. minced onion
1-1/2 tsp. powdered ginger
1/2 tsp. red pepper flakes
3/4 c. lemon juice
1 c. Sultana or Golden raisins

(more)

(continued)

Put peaches in large bowl and cover with brine made of the coarse salt and 4 cups water. Let stand overnight, then drain thoroughly. Using a large saucepan, combine 1/4 c. water, the sugar, cider vinegar and garlic and bring to a boil. Add peaches, cover and simmer until fruit is translucent. With slotted spoon, remove peaches from syrup and set aside. To mixture in saucepan, add onion, powdered ginger, red pepper flakes, lemon juice and raisins and cook uncovered until thickened 15 to 20 minutes. Add peaches and candied ginger, return to boil and immediately ladle into hot sterilized jars. Seal and store in cool, dark place.

PEACH SAUCE

3 peaches, peeled or
  3 c. frozen peach slices
1 c. fresh-squeezed orange juice
2 T. cornstarch
1/4 tsp. ground nutmeg

(more)

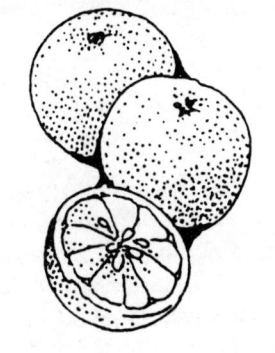

(continued)

If using fresh peaches, slice two of them. Set aside. Coarsely chop the remaining peach. For frozen fruit, set aside 2 cups. Pour the orange juice into a blender. Add the chopped peach or 1 cup of the sliced frozen peaches. Blend until smooth. Pour into a saucepan; add the cornstarch and nutmeg. Cook, stirring constantly, until thickened. Add the remaining sliced peaches. Heat through. Serve warm.

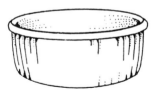

SHALLOT AND PEACH CHUTNEY

Makes 3-1/4 cups (allow about 2 T. per serving).

3 c. peaches (or papaya or mango)
3 oz. shallots, peeled & thinly sliced
1-1/2 c. cider vinegar
1/4 c. lemon juice
1 c. brown sugar, packed

1/2 c. golden raisins
1 T. fresh minced ginger
2 cloves garlic, minced
1/2 tsp. salt
1/2 tsp. ground cinnamon

(more)

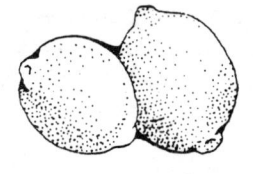

(continued)

In a large saucepan, combine the peaches (or papaya or mango), shallots, vinegar and lemon juice. Bring to boiling; reduce heat. Simmer, stirring occasionally, for 5 minutes. Add remaining ingredients in pan; simmer, stirring frequently. for 15 minutes. Cool; spoon into refrigerator or freezer containers. Cover and chill. Serve chilled or at room temperature with roasts, barbecued meats. on burgers or with fish.

SWEET AND SPICY PEACH RELISH

4 large ripe or semi-ripe peaches, pitted and thinly sliced
1 green bell pepper, cut into thin strips
1/2 c. orange juice
6 T. lime juice (about 3 limes)
1 T. minced red or green chili pepper of your choice
1 tsp. minced garlic
1 red bell pepper, cut into thin strips
1 red onion, peeled and very thinly sliced
1/4 c. virgin olive oil
1 T. molasses
1/2 c. chopped Italian or curly parsley
Salt and fresh cracked pepper

In a large bowl, combine all the ingredients and mix well. This relish will keep covered and refrigerated about 4 days. Makes about 4 cups.

TOMATO-PEACH BARBECUE SAUCE

2 c. peeled, pitted and
    chopped peaches
1/2 c. apple cider vinegar
1/4 c. vegetable oil
1 T. dry mustard
1/2 tsp. salt
1/2 tsp. pepper

1 (10-3/4 oz.) can tomato soup,
    undiluted
1/2 c. firmly packed brown sugar
1/2 c. light corn syrup
2 T. Worcestershire sauce
1 T. paprika
1/2 tsp. garlic powder

Combine all ingredients in a heavy 2-quart saucepan; bring to a boil, stirring constantly. Cover, reduce heat and simmer 25 minutes, stirring occasionally. Yields 2 quarts.

PICKLED PEACHES

1 pint cooked peach halves

To the syrup add: 3/4 c. firmly packed brown sugar, 1/2 c. vinegar, two 3" sticks of cinnamon, 1 tsp. whole cloves, 1 tsp. all spice. Boil for 5 minutes.

Add the peach halves and simmer for another 5 minutes. Chill in syrup several hours or overnight. Quick and easy and delicious with meats or on a party plate.

PEACH BUTTER

10 c. peach pulp   3 T. lemon juice
7 c. sugar

Peel and mash peaches to make 10 cups of peach pulp. Boil peach pulp and lemon juice for 5 minutes. Add sugar and cook 20 minutes or until thick. Seal in jars.

SPICED PEACHES

7 lbs. prepared fruit   1 crushed nutmeg
1 qt. cider vinegar   1 dozen whole cloves
3 lbs. granulated sugar   Cinnamon bark

Put sugar in the vinegar and add the spices tied in a bag. When sugar is dissolved, add the fruit and boil until tender.

CANNED HONEY PEACHES

3 c. water   1/2 c. sugar
1/2 c. honey   12 peaches

Boil water and sugar for 5 minutes; add honey. Scald peaches in boiling
water to loosen skins; peel, cut in halves and remove stones. Cook fruit
in syrup for 5 to 10 minutes until tender with fork. Arrange peaches with
cut side down in jar. Fill to overflowing with hot syrup and remove air
bubbles with sterilized knife. Cover with lid just taken from boiling water.

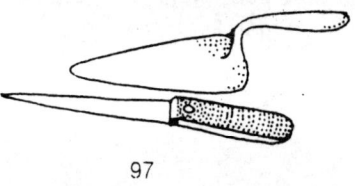

PEACH SALADS

FRUIT SALAD

29 oz. sliced peaches
15-1/2 oz. can pineapple chunks
11 oz. can mandarin orange
   segments
3 c. liquid (juice from fruits plus
   enough water to make 3 cups

1 (3 oz.) pkg. vanilla pudding
   mix, not instant
1 (3 oz.) pkg. tapioca pudding
   mix, not instant

Drain fruit (keep juice). Stir and combine pudding mixes and 3 c. liquid. Microwave on full power until it boils (about 6 to 8 minutes) and turns clear and thick. Cool and add drained fruit. Keeps well in refrigerator. Optional: Add bananas, fresh strawberries, etc.

PEACH COTTAGE CHEESE SALAD

1 (3 oz.) box peach Jello (dry)   9 oz. carton Cool Whip
1 small carton cottage cheese   1 c. peaches

Cut peaches in bite sizes. Mix with Jello and cottage cheese. Last, fold
in Cool Whip.

100

PEACH SALAD

1 pkg. peach Jello
1 pkg. vanilla pudding (not instant)

1 c. peaches, save juice and
add enough water for 2 cups

Cook Jello, pudding and 2 c. of juice until it comes to a good boil, then let set until firm. Add a small container of Cool Whip and peach slices.

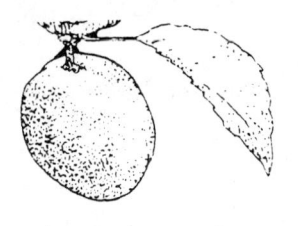

PEACHY BANANA SALAD

1 (1 lb.) can sliced peaches
1 (3 oz.) pkg. peach gelatin
   in juice & water (1 cup)

1 container of peach yogurt
1 sliced banana

Pour the juice off can of sliced peaches; add enough water to make 1 cup. Bring to a boil. Dissolve 1 pkg. of peach gelatin in the hot liquid. Add 1 container of peach yogurt and stir until thoroughly combined. Chill until slightly thickened. Add the can of peaches and sliced banana. Chill until firm.

102

PEACH PUDDINGS

EASY BAKED PEACH PUDDING

(Preheat oven to 350°.)

1 pt. sliced, peeled peaches	1/4 c. butter
2 T. flour	1 egg
1/4 tsp. salt	1 tsp. vanilla
1 c. sugar	

Place peaches in a 1-qt. casserole. Mix sugar, flour and salt. Work butter into dry mixture. Add well beaten egg and vanilla. Mix and pour over peaches, spooning through the fruit. Bake at 350° until fruit is tender and browned, approximately 30 to 45 minutes.

ELEGANT AND CREAMY PEACH PUDDING

3 c. cooked rice (brown short grain)
3 c. milk
1/4 c. sugar
1 tsp. vanilla
1/4 c. rice syrup

2 T. margarine
2 tsp. lemon juice
1 tsp. grated lemon peel
1/2 tsp. ground nutmeg
1/8 tsp. salt (optional)

(more)

(continued)

Combine rice milk and sugar in 3-qt. saucepan and cook over medium heat until thick and creaming, stirring often (25 minutes). Add vanilla. Pour into 4-qt. serving bowl. Heat syrup, margarine, lemon juice/peel, nutmeg and salt. Stir in peaches and cook on low for 10 minutes. Spoon over rice pudding. Serve warm or cold. Makes 10 servings.

106

BAKED PEACH PUDDING

(Preheat oven to 325°.)

2 c. sliced peaches
3/4 c. sugar
1/2 c. milk
4 T. oleo
1 T. baking powder

1 c. flour
1 c. sugar
1 T. cornstarch
1/4 tsp. salt
1 c. boiling water

Layer peaches in greased 10x10-inch dish. Combine sugar, milk, oleo, baking powder and flour and pour over peaches. Combine sugar, cornstarch, salt and spread over the above mixture. Pour over slowly the boiling water and bake for 50 minutes at 325°. Serve warm with Half and Half.

PEACH MOUSSE

2 c. ripe peach pulp
2 c. heavy cream
1/2 c. Confectioner's sugar
24 vanilla wafers or lady fingers,
   crushed

1/2 tsp. almond
Few grains of salt
4 egg whites

Mix peach pulp with cream, sugar, vanilla and salt. Fold in stiffly beaten egg whites; place in refrigerator tray. When mixture starts to thicken, fold in wafer crumbs, saving 1/2 c. to sprinkle over top of mixture. Place in refrigerator for several hours.

PEACHIE PUDDING BAKE

8 medium peaches	1 c. Bisquick
3/4 c. brown sugar	1/4 tsp. nutmeg

Peel peaches and slice into a large bowl. Sprinkle evenly with sugar and let stand 10 minutes. Stir in Bisquick and nutmeg. Turn fruit into greased nonmetallic baking dish. Micro-cook on roast temperature for 15 minutes. Serve with ice cream. Makes 6 servings.

PEACH TAPIOCA

3 c. sliced cooked peaches   1/2 c. sugar
3 c. hot water   1 tsp. lemon extract
1/2 c. minute tapioca

Blend tapioca and sugar, stir in water. Cook in double boiler until clear, about 20 minutes. Add lemon. Pour over peaches. Serve cold with custard sauce.

PEACH ICE CREAMS AND ICE CREAM TOPPINGS

PEACH CUSTARD ICE CREAM

3 eggs, large
1-1/2 c. sugar
2 c. peaches, peeled and
   coarsely chopped
1 tsp. vanilla

2 T. flour
2 c. milk
1 T. lemon juice
1-1/2 c. whipping cream

(more)

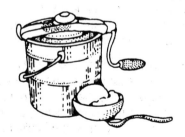

112

In a large bowl, beat the eggs to blend. In a 3-4 quart saucepan, whisk flour, 1 cup of the sugar and milk until smooth. Stir often over medium-high heat until boiling, about 8 minutes. Whisking rapidly, pour hot sauce into eggs. (This will destroy any salmonella bacteria.) In a blender, smoothly puree peaches with lemon juice and remaining 1/2 c. sugar.

Stir into cooked mixture and chill, covered, until cold 2 hours or up to a day. Stir in cream and vanilla. Freeze peach mixture in a regular or self-refrigerated ice cream maker according to manufacturer's directions. Serve when softly frozen or package airtight and store in freezer up to 2 weeks. Let soften at room temperature about 10 minutes before scooping. Makes 1-1/2 quarts.

PEACH ICE CREAM

3 c. mashed fresh peaches
1 T. lemon juice
1 qt. milk
3 c. whipping cream
1-1/2 c. sugar

1 tsp. vanilla extract
1/4 tsp. almond extract
1/4 tsp. salt
2 drops red food coloring

Combine peaches and lemon juice. Sweeten mashed peaches to taste. Combine milk, cream, sugar, vanilla and almond extracts, and salt in large bowl. Add peaches to mixture. Stir in food coloring. Chill. Churn-freeze. Three cans (1 lb. each) peaches. drained and mashed, can be substituted for fresh peaches. Makes 1 gallon.

PEACH ICE CREAM CUSTARD

Make a custard of:

1 quart cream	2 quarts ripe peaches
1 pint milk	(mashed and sweetened)
3 eggs, beaten	1 T. vanilla
1 c. sugar	

Beat eggs, stir in sugar, milk and one half of cream. Cook in double boiler until mixture thickens as custard. Chill. Stir in cream, partly freeze, then stir in sweetened and strained peaches. Use from freezer.

PEACH ICE CREAM
(Electric Refrigerator)

2 tsp. gelatin
1/2 c. cold water
1-3/4 c. evaporated milk, scald
1/2 c. sugar

2 tsp. vanilla
1-1/2 c. whipped cream
1 c. mashed sweetened peach
    pulp

Soften gelatin in cold water. Pour into hot milk. Cool. Add sugar, vanilla and peach pulp; blend well. Chill. Pour into freezing tray. When mixture thickens fold in whipped cream. After 1 hour use rotary beater and beat mixture in a chilled bowl. Pour into freezing tray, another 3 to 4 hours.

BAKED PEACHES
Low Fat

(Preheat oven to 450°.)

1 lb. peach slices,
    thawed if frozen
2 c. vanilla fat-free ice cream

1/2 c. sugar
2 tsp. unsalted butter

Arrange peaches in a glass baking dish. Sprinkle with sugar. Dot peaches with butter. Bake 15 to 25 minutes, basting peaches occasionally, until tender. Serve peaches over ice cream.

CINNAMON PEACHES

Microwaveable

4 peaches, ripe, peeled & halved
1/4 c. white dry wine
1/4 tsp. ground cinnamon
Fresh berries

2 T. brown sugar, firmly packed
1 tsp. lemon juice
Yogurt

Place peach halves in a microwave casserole. Combine the wine, cinnamon, brown sugar and lemon juice. Pour over the peaches. Cover tightly and microwave on high for 2 minutes. Turn peaches over and microwave covered for 3 minutes. Cool. Serve with yogurt and berries.

FRIED PEACHES

8 large peaches
3 T. butter

1 T. dark brown sugar
Vanilla ice cream

Peel, halve the peaches and remove seeds. Cut thin slice off rounded side of peach to level. Melt the butter in a large skillet and put in the peaches, leveled side down. Fill hollows with brown sugar. Simmer, covered until just beginning to get soft. Serve with a scoop of vanilla ice cream on top of each peach half.

STUFFED PEACHES

Serves 4

4 large peaches
2 T. lemon juice
1/4 c. chopped raisins
1 T. honey

(more)

1 tsp. vanilla extract
1 tsp. grated lemon rind
1/2 tsp. ground cinnamon
1/2 c. low-fat yogurt

(continued)

Scald peaches in boiling water for 1 minute to loosen skins. Drain, peel, cut in half and discard the pits. Brush the fruit with lemon juice to prevent discoloration. With a grapefruit spoon or melon scoop, remove about half of the pulp from each peach, leaving a sturdy shell. Brush the insides of the shells with more lemon juice. Chop the pulp. In small bowl, combine the raisins, honey, vanilla, lemon rind and cinnamon. Add the peach pulp. Fold in just enough yogurt to bind the stuffing together. Divide the stuffing among the peach halves. Serve immediately.

PEACH CRISP

THIRTY MINUTE PEACH CRISP

(Preheat oven to 400°.)

32 oz. sliced peaches,
  well drained
1/2 c. all purpose flour
1/3 c. chopped dry roasted peanuts
1/2 c. margarine or butter

1/4 c. raisins
1 (3-3/4 oz.) pkg. butterscotch
  flavored instant pudding mix
1/4 c. rolled oats

In 8-inch square baking dish place peaches and raisins; set aside. In small bowl combine remaining ingredients; cut in margarine until crumbly. Sprinkle over peaches and raisins. Bake for 15 to 20 minutes or until bubbly around edges.

PEACH CARAMEL CRISP

You'll need a 9-inch oven-proof short-sided baking dish.

PRALINE TOPPING:
1/2 c. sugar
1 c. sliced almonds, toasted
5 T. unsalted butter

3 T. water
1/2 c. all purpose flour

PEACHES:
1/2 c. sugar
6 large ripe peaches,
   peeled, pitted and cut into
   8 wedges each

3 T. water
2 T. cornstarch

(more)

124

(continued)

TOPPING:
Butter small cookie sheet. Stir sugar and water in heavy saucepan over low heat until dissolved. Increase heat and boil without stirring until sugar turns a dark golden color. Mix in almonds. Immediately pour mixture onto greased cookie sheet. Allow to cool completely. Crack into pieces and grind fine in a food processor.

(more)

125

(continued)

NOTE: You can prepare the praline ahead; store in an airtight container and refrigerate up to 2 weeks. This recipe makes more praline than required for one dish, so you can store it and make another crisp weeks later.

Set the oven for 375°. Combine 1/2 c. praline and flour in food processor. Add cold butter and pulse on and off until mixture is crumbly. Set aside.

In a heavy saucepan, stir sugar and water over low heat until dissolved. Increase heat and boil without stirring.

PEACH COOKIE CRISP

(Preheat oven to 375°.)

6 c. sliced peaches
1/3 c. minute tapioca
Squeeze of lemon juice
Grated lemon rind
1/2 tsp. cinnamon
Little salt

1-1/4 c. all purpose flour
3/4 c. brown sugar
1 c. cookie crumbs
1/2 c. chopped almonds or
   pecans
3/4 c. butter or margarine

Mix the first 6 ingredients and put into a 9x13-inch baking dish. Mix the next 5 ingredients with a fork and put on top of the peach mixture. Bake for 40 minutes.

PEACH FRUIT CRISP

(Preheat oven to 350°.)

5 to 6 c. sliced fruit
   Peaches, nectarines,
   plums, apples
2 T. lemon juice
1/2 c. sugar

1 c. flour
1 c. oats
1 tsp. ground cinnamon
1/2 c. brown sugar, packed
1/2 c. butter (cut into pats)

(more)

128

(continued)

Place fruit in 8-inch square baking dish. Sprinkle with lemon juice and sugar. Combine flour, oats, cinnamon and brown sugar. Cut in butter with pastry blender or fingers until mixture is crumbly. Sprinkle over fruit. Bake at 350° for 35 to 40 minutes until crumbs are golden brown and fruit is tender when pierced with a knife. Top with ice cream or Cool Whip. 1/4 c. chopped nuts may be added to topping mixture. Makes 6 to 8 servings.

PEACH YUMMY CRISP

(Preheat oven to 325°.)

29 oz. sliced peaches
1 pkg. butter brickle cake mix
  (or yellow cake mix)

1 c. coconut
1 c. nuts
1/2 c. melted margarine

Pour peaches with syrup into ungreased 9x13-inch pan. Sprinkle with cake mix, then coconut and nuts. Pour on the melted margarine. Bake for 55 to 60 minutes.

PEACH BEVERAGES

GOTCHA PEACH PUNCH

8 ripe peaches
2 bottles dry white wine (chilled)
4 maraschino cherries

Pour boiling water over the peaches and let stand about 3/4 minute. Remove peaches with slotted spoon. Skins will peel off readily.

(more)

(continued)

Put peaches into a clear glass pitcher. Pour wine over peaches immediately to prevent discoloration. Refrigerate for 3 hours so peaches will flavor the wine.

To serve, place pitcher on the dinner table. As wine is poured, add additional chilled wine.

Peaches can be served sliced over vanilla pudding or ice cream for an elegant dessert.

PEACH MELOMEL

6 lbs. peaches
2-1/2 lb. acacia honey
Graves yeast
1/4 oz. malic acid

3/4 pint elderflowers
1/30 ounce tannin
1/4 oz. tartaric acid

(more)

(continued)

Press peaches (after removing pits). Dissolve honey in 4 pints warm water, blend in peach juice along with acid, tannin and nutrients. Add 100 ppm sulfite (2 campden tablets). After 24 hours add yeast starter, allow to ferment 7 days before adding elderflowers. Ferment on flowers for 3 days, then strain off flowers and top off to 1 gallon with cold water. Ferment until specific gravity drops to 10, then rack. Rack again when gravity drops to 5, and add 1 tablet campden. Rack again when a heavy deposit forms, or after 3 months, whichever comes first. Add another campden tablet. Rack again every 3-4 months, adding a tablet after every second racking.

PEACH WINE

2-1/2 lbs. peaches (about 10 peaches)
7 pints water
   sugar TO SG=1.100 (about 2 lb.)
1 Campden tablet
1-1/2 tsp. acid blend
1 tsp. pectic enzyme powder
1/2 tsp. yeast energizer
1/4 tsp. tannin
1 pkg. wine yeast

(more)

136

(continued)

Wash peaches, quarter, remove stones and any brown patches. You can leave the skin on and remove all of the reddish meat around the stones. Place peach quarters in nylon straining bag and place in primary. Crush peaches, extracting as much juice as possible. Add dry ingredients to primary except yeast. Add hot (tap hot works fine) water and mix thoroughly. Cover and let set for 24 hours. After 24 hours, add wine yeast. Ferment for 3 to 5 days (SG=1.040). Rack into secondary and attach lock. Rack in 3 weeks and again in 3 months.

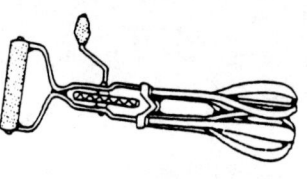

YOGUR-TEA PEACH SHAKE

A frothy, refreshing treat.

1/3 c. Diet Natural Lemon Flavored Ice Tea mix
1 pint (16 oz.) vanilla yogurt
1-1/2 c. cold water
3 peaches or nectarines, peeled and quartered

In blender, combine all ingredients; process at
high speed until blended. Serve with ice and
garnish, if desired, with peach slices. Makes
about 5 servings.

PEACH AND CHAMPAGNE SPECIAL

1 pint frozen vanilla yogurt
1/2 c. fresh peaches
1 kiwi, peeled and sliced

1 split chilled champagne
(2 cups)

Mix yogurt, champagne and peaches
together until smooth and creamy. Pour
into wine glasses and serve immediately
garnished with kiwi slices.

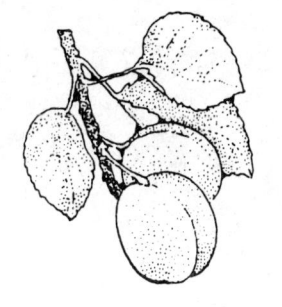

AFTER SCHOOL PEACH SHAKE

1 c. fresh peaches
1 c. plain yogurt
1 T. honey or sugar
1/2 tsp. vanilla

Blend in blender until smooth.
Yield 2 cups.

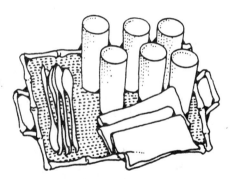

PEACH DAIQUIRI

2-1/2 oz. light rum
1/2 fresh peach, peeled
1/2 oz. lime juice

1 tsp. sugar
1 c. crushed ice

Put all ingredients in a blender and blend until thick and smooth. Serve immediately in a large saucer champagne glass, with a short straw. Makes 1 serving.

FRUIT-TEA REFRESHER

The slightly crushed fruit adds great flavor.

2 medium peaches, sliced
1/2 c. Diet Natural Lemon Flavor
    Iced Tea Mix

1 medium orange, sliced
1-1/2 qts. cold water

In large pitcher, combine fruit with diet natural lemon flavor iced tea mix, crushing fruit slightly. Stir in water; chill at least 2 hours. Makes about 6 servings.

PEACH DESSERTS

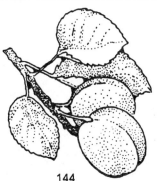

BAKED FRUIT DISH

(Preheat oven to 350°.)

2 T. cornstarch (heaping)
1 c. powdered sugar (heaping)
16 oz. can pears
16 oz. can peaches

16 oz. can chunk pineapple
16 oz. can apricots
1 dozen prunes
Maraschino cherries

Drain all fruit. Arrange in 9x13-inch casserole. Sprinkle powdered sugar and cornstarch mixture over fruit. Tab 1 stick butter or oleo over top. Garnish with cherries. Bake for 45 to 50 minutes.

FRESH PEACH DESSERT

CRUST:
1 c. flour   1/4 c. powdered sugar
1/2 c. butter or margarine

FILLING:
1 c. sugar   2 T. white corn syrup
1 c. water   2 T. (rounded) peach Jello
4 T. cornstarch   2 c. fresh peaches (peeled and sliced)

Make, bake and cool crust. Cook sugar, cornstarch, water and syrup until thick. Add peach Jello and cool, covered. Does not need to be completely cold. Stir in peaches and pour over crust. Makes a 9x9-inch pan. Serve with dollop of Cool Whip.

FROZEN DESSERT

2 c. whipped cream
1 c. peach pie filling or
   2-1/2 c. peaches with juice,
   thickened

1 c. drained fruit cocktail
1 tsp. almond flavoring
1 pkg. small marshmallows

Fold together. Put in a 9x12-inch pan and sprinkle moist coconut on top. Refrigerate or freeze.

FROZEN FRUIT CUPS

2 c. sugar
1 c. water
1 qt. frozen or fresh strawberries

1 qt. peaches (drained and sliced)
6 to 8 bananas (diced) or you may
   use your choice of fruits

Boil sugar and water together until clear. Cool and set aside. Mix fruits together in a pan or bowl, pouring cooled syrup over it. Blend together. Put into fruit cups for individual servings and freeze. Serve while still frozen.

148

FRUIT CHEDDAR BARS

(Preheat oven to 375°.)

2-3/4 c. unbleached flour	2-1/2 c. sharp cheddar, shredded
1 tsp. baking powder	2 large eggs, beaten
3/4 c. butter	1/2 c. peach preserves
1/2 c. strawberry preserves	(See pgs. 72-76)

Sift the dry ingredients together and cut in the butter until the pieces are the size of peas. Add the cheese and toss lightly. Add the eggs and blend well. Chill one quarter of the dough. Press the remaining dough into the bottom and sides of an ungreased 15x10x1/2-inch jelly roll pan.

(more)

(continued)

Spread half the dough with the peach preserves and the other half with the strawberry preserves. Roll the chilled dough on a lightly floured surface to 1/4-inch thick. Cut the dough into 1/2-inch strips and place the strips diagonally across the top of the preserves making a lattice of the strips. Press the ends of the dough against the side dough to seal. Bake in the preheated oven for 35 minutes or until lightly browned. Cool before cutting into 2x3-inch bars.

FRUIT REFRIGERATOR DESSERT

1 small box vanilla wafers.
  (20 to 30 wafers)
1/2 c. butter
1-1/2 c. powdered sugar
2 eggs

1 c. whipped cream
2 c. thickened fruit.
  (blueberries, strawberries,
  drained canned pineapple,
  fresh peaches)

Crush wafers and spread half on bottom of pan. Cream butter, powdered sugar and eggs together well. Alternate layers of fruit, creamed mixture and whipped cream and top with remainder of crushed wafer crumbs. Refrigerate for a few hours.

PEACH AND CHERRY TART WITH ALMOND PASTE

(Preheat oven to 375°.)

Blend together:

1 c. almond paste	1 egg, lightly beaten
Sugar, to taste	Almond extract, to taste
(couple of tablespoons)	(a splash)

Into a pie plate, fit a pastry for a single crust pie (either frozen or your own). Spread the almond filling into the bottom.

Add:

4 ripe peach halves	1 c. dark red cherries, stemmed and pitted

Brush with 2 T. melted butter. Sprinkle with a little almond extract and about 2 T. sugar. Bake about 1 hour until golden and tender.

PEACH CHEESE DESSERT

1 c. + 2 T. flour
1 c. chopped nuts
1/4 c. brown sugar
1 stick margarine (melted)
8 oz. cream cheese
1/2 c. powdered sugar
1 tsp. vanilla

2 c. Cool Whip
1-1/2 c. water
1/4 c. sugar
2 T. cornstarch
3 oz. peach Jello
4 c. peaches (sliced)

Mix the first 4 ingredients and press into 9x13-inch pan. Bake 15 minutes at 350°. Cool. Mix softened cheese, sugar, vanilla and Cool Whip. Spread over crust and chill. Cook water, sugar and cornstarch until thick. Add Jello and sliced peaches. Pour over and chill.

PEACH DELIGHT

Fresh peaches
1 c. sugar
1 c. flour

1 tsp. baking powder
1/4 tsp. salt
1/2 c. butter or margarine

Slice fresh peaches in pan. Mix together the sugar, flour, baking powder, salt and butter. Sprinkle over fruit and bake in moderate oven for about 30 minutes. Serve with cream or ice cream.

PEACH DESSERT

3 egg whites
1 c. white sugar
17 soda crackers
1/4 c. coarse walnuts

1 tsp. vanilla
1 large can peaches (sliced)
Cool Whip

Beat egg whites until stiff, gradually add sugar and beat again until very stiff. Crumble soda crackers (not too fine). Add crackers, walnuts and vanilla to egg whites and sugar mixture. Spread mixture in a greased 9x13-inch pan and bake at 350° for 25 to 30 minutes. Let cool. Drain peach slices, pat dry and cut in chunks. Fold in Cool Whip and spread on crust. Refrigerate overnight.

PEACH DESSERT - EASY WAY

(Preheat oven to 325°.)

1 large can peaches
1 pkg. yellow cake mix

1 c. brown sugar
1 stick margarine (melted)

Place peaches in large Pyrex dish (may cut peaches if desired). Put dry cake mix on top of peaches. Sprinkle brown sugar on top of cake mix. Pour melted margarine evenly on top of brown sugar. Bake for 50 to 60 minutes or until brown.

PEACH MELBA
Low Fat

6 peach halves
1/3 c. low fat vanilla yogurt
1/2 c. raspberries, pureed
Sugar subs. if needed

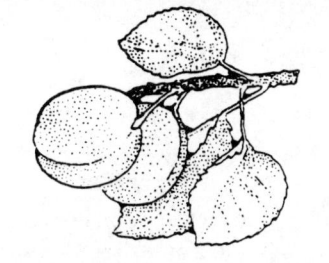

Place each peach half in a serving dish. Spoon about 1 T. yogurt over each peach half. Pour on the raspberry puree. Add sugar substitute before serving if the puree needs to be sweetened. Yield 6 servings.

PEACH-NECTARINE GRATIN WITH SUGARED ALMOND TOPPING

(Preheat oven to 425°.)

Butter a 9-inch pie plate with 2 T. butter. Sprinkle with 2 T. sugar.

Peel, pit and halve 6 to 8 peaches and nectarines Place fruit cut side down in the butter and sugar.

For the batter, mix together:
1 egg
1/4 c. milk
1/4 c. flour
1/8 tsp. salt

Pour the batter over the fruit.

(more)

158

(continued)

For the topping, mix together:

4 T. sugar   4 T. chopped almonds

Sprinkle the topping over the fruit and the batter, and then dot with 1 T. butter. Bake 15 minutes. Serve warm.

PEACH PLUM GRATIN

(Preheat oven to 375°.)

2 tsp. fresh ginger, grated
3/4 lb. plums, pitted and cut
  into thick slices
2 T. sugar
2 c. vanilla frozen yogurt

1 lb. peaches, peeled, pitted
  and cut into thick slices
1 c. apple cider
1/2 c. almond cookies, crumbled

(more)

Sprinkle ginger in the bottom of a shallow baking dish. Alternate layers of peaches and plums over ginger. Pour cider over fruit. Sprinkle with sugar and crumbled almond cookies. Bake 45 to 50 minutes or until fruit mixture is syrupy. Serve fruit with frozen yogurt.

QUICK PEACH DESSERT

4 peaches, sliced
1/2 c. sugar
4 sponge cake shells
1 c. light frozen dessert topping

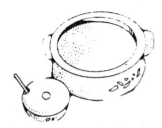

Combine peaches and sugar in a bowl. Refrigerate 20 to 30 minutes for sugar to dissolve. Stir well before spooning into cake shells. Serve with a dollop of dessert topping.

QUICK PEACH PECAN DESSERT

(Preheat oven to 325°.)

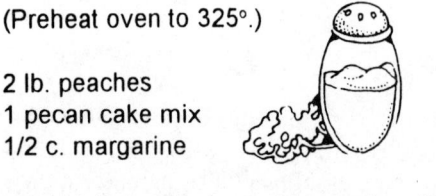

2 lb. peaches
1 pecan cake mix
1/2 c. margarine

1 c. coconut
1/2 c. pecans (or more)

In 9x13-inch pan, layer the peaches (including syrup); then spread out the cake mix (dry) on top. Then melt the margarine and drizzle on top. Sprinkle the coconut on top, then sprinkle the chopped pecans on top of everything. Bake for 55 minutes until brown on top.

PEACH YUMMIES

PEACH CREME

4 lbs. peaches, sliced, thawed if frozen
2 c. lowfat lemon yogurt
1/2 tsp. vanilla extract
4 shortbread cookies

Combine peaches, yogurt and vanilla in
a bowl. Serve with cookies.

PEACHES-N-CREAM

(Preheat oven to 350°.)

3/4 c. flour
1 tsp. baking powder
1/2 tsp. salt
1 box dry vanilla pudding (not instant)

3 T. soft butter
1 egg
1/2 c. milk

TOPPING:
8 oz. cream cheese
3 T. peach juice

1/2 c. sugar

Combine first 7 ingredients and beat for 2 minutes. Pour into greased 10-inch pie plate. Put 15 oz. can drained peaches over. For Topping: Beat 2 minutes, spoon to within 1 inch of edge of batter. Sprinkle with 1 T. sugar and 1/2 tsp. of cinnamon. Bake for 30 to 35 minutes. Good warm!

PEACH MUFFINS

(Preheat oven to 375°.)

1/2 c. butter, room temperature
2 large eggs
2 tsp. baking powder
2-1/2 c. peaches
   (mash 1/2 c. with a fork)
1 T. sugar mixed with 1/4 tsp.
   ground nutmeg

1 c. granulated sugar
1 tsp. vanilla extract
1/4 tsp. salt
2 c. all purpose flour
1/2 c. milk

(more)

(continued)

Grease 12 regular muffin cups, including the area between each cup or use foil baking cups. In a medium-size bowl, beat butter until creamy. Beat in sugar until pale and fluffy. Beat in eggs, one at a time. Beat in vanilla, baking powder and salt. Mix mashed peaches into batter. Fold in half the flour with a spatula, then half the milk. Add remaining flour and milk. Fold in remaining peaches. Scoop batter into muffin cups. Sprinkle with nutmeg sugar. Bake 25 to 30 minutes or until golden brown. Let muffins cool at least 30 minutes in the pan before removing.

RIVER PEACH PUFF

(Preheat oven to 350°.)

1-1/2 c. milk	1/2 c. sugar
2 c. bread cubes	1 tsp. vanilla extract
2 T. melted butter or margarine	1/8 tsp. salt
2 eggs (beaten)	1 tsp. grated lemon peel
1/4 c. honey	2 c. chopped peaches

Scald milk and pour over bread cubes. Set aside for 10 minutes. Add melted butter, eggs, honey, sugar, vanilla, salt and lemon peel. Mix well and stir in peaches. Pour into greased 8-inch square baking pan or dish. Bake about 45 minutes or until golden brown. Serve with ice cream or whipped cream. This will serve 4-6.

Are you up a stump for some nice gifts for some nice people in your life? Well, don't forget HEARTS'N TUMMIES COOKBOOKS. Here's a list of some of the best cookbooks in the western half of the Universe. Just check 'em off, stick a check in an envelope with this page, and we'll get your books off to you pronto. Oh, yes, add $2.00 for shipping and handling. If you order over $25.00 worth, forget the shipping and handling Here they are! **Mini Cookbooks**

(Only 3-1/2 x 5) With Maxi Good Eatin -- 160 or 192 pages -- $5.95

☐ Arkansas Cooking
☐ Dakota Cooking
☐ Illinois Cooking
☐ Indiana Cooking
☐ Iowa Cookin'
☐ Kansas Cookin'
☐ Michigan Cooking
☐ Minnesota Cookin'
☐ Missouri Cookin'
☐ New Jersey Cooking
☐ New York Cooking
☐ Ohio Cooking
☐ Pennsylvania Cooking
☐ Wisconsin Cooking
☐ Aphrodisiac Cooking
☐ Apples! Apples! Apples!

☐ Apples Galore
☐ Berries! Berries! Berries!
☐ Cherries! Cherries! Cherries!
☐ Citrus! Citrus! Citrus!
☐ Cooking with Fresh Herbs
☐ Cooking with Spirits
☐ Cooking with Garlic
☐ Cooking with Things Go Cluck
☐ Cooking with Things Go Moo
☐ Cooking with Things Go Oink
☐ Cooking with Things Go Splash
☐ Cape Cod Cooking
☐ Good Cookin' From the
Plain People
☐ Hill Country Cookin'

☐ Kid Cookin'
☐ The Kid's Garden Fun Book
☐ Kid Pumpkin Fun Book
☐ Midwest Small Town Cookin'
☐ Muffins Cookbook
☐ Nuts! Nuts! Nuts!
☐ Off To College Cookbook
☐ Peaches! Peaches! Peaches!
☐ Pregnant Lady Cooking
☐ Pumpkins! Pumpkins! Pumpkins!

☐ Super Simple Cookin'
☐ Working Girl Cookbook
☐ Veggie Talk Coloring &
Story Book $6.95

In Between Cookbooks
(5 1/2 x 8 1/2) - 150 pages - $9.95

- ☐ The Adaptable Apple Cookbook
- ☐ Breads! Breads! Breads!
- ☐ Camp Cookin'
- ☐ Cooking Ala Nude
- ☐ The Cow Puncher's Cookbook
- ☐ Eating Ohio
- ☐ Farmers Market Cookbook
- ☐ The Fire Fighters Cookbook
- ☐ Halloween Fun Book
- ☐ Herbal Cookery
- ☐ Hunting in the Nude Cookbook
- ☐ Ice Cream Cookbook
- ☐ Wil-kon-ge Inizan Maazina 'Igans (The Indian Moon Cookbook)
- ☐ Indian Cooking Cookbook
- ☐ Mad About Garlic
- ☐ Motorcycler's Wild Critter Cookbook
- ☐ Soccer Mom's Cookbook
- ☐ Shhhh Cookbook
- ☐ Vegan Vegetarian Cookbook

Biggie Cookbooks
(5-1/2 x 8-1/2) - 200 plus pages - $11.95

- ☐ A Cookbook for them what Ain't Done a Whole lot of Cookin'
- ☐ Aphrodisiac Cooking
- ☐ Back to the Supper Table Cookbook
- ☐ Cooking for One (ok, Maybe two)
- ☐ Covered Bridges Cookbook
- ☐ Depression Times Cookbook
- ☐ Dial-a-Dream Cookbook
- ☐ Flat out, Dirt Cheap Cookin'
- ☐ Hormone Helper Cookbook
- ☐ The I-got-Funner-things-to-do-than-cook Cookbook
- ☐ Lake Country Cookbook
- ☐ Mississippi River Cookin'
- ☐ The Orchard, Berry Patches and Gardens Cookbook
- ☐ Roarin' 20's Cookbook
- ☐ Wild Critter Cookbook

☐ The Body Shop (A Low-Fat Cookbook) $14.95

Hearts 'N Tummies Cookbook Co.
1854 - 345th Ave
Wever, IA 52658
800-571-2665